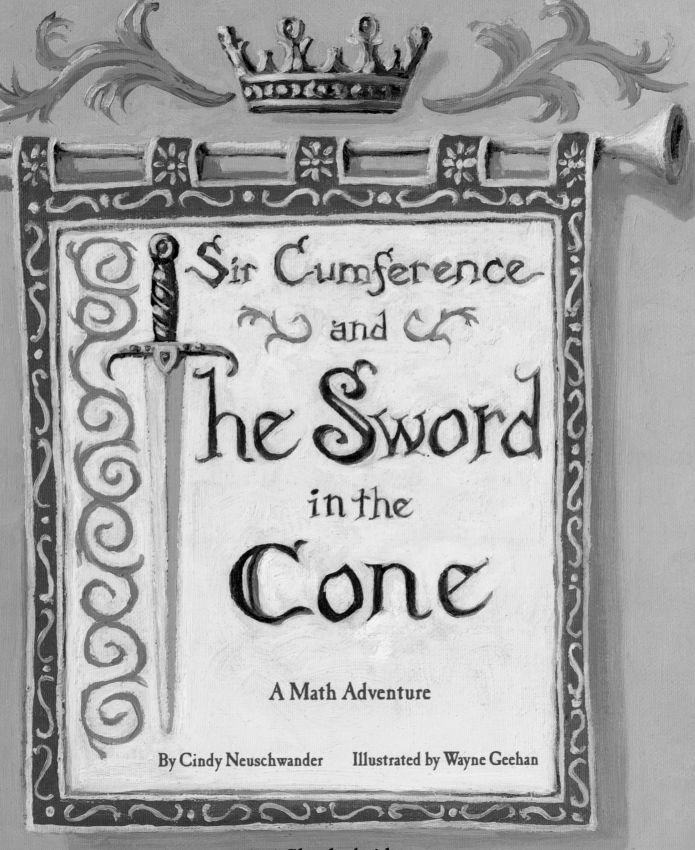

Sir Cumference and The Sword in the Cone

A Math Adventure

By Cindy Neuschwander   Illustrated by Wayne Geehan

Charlesbridge

For Seth, who soars on wings
like an eagle. Keep
running! — C.N.

For my wife Susan — W.G.

Published by Charlesbridge, 85 Main Street, Watertown, MA 02472
(617) 926-0329 • www.charlesbridge.com

Printed in Korea
(hc) 10 9 8 7   (sc) 20 19 18 17 16 15 14 13 12 11

Library of Congress Cataloging-in-Publication Data
Neuschwander, Cindy.
    Sir Cumference and the sword in the cone / by Cindy Neuschwander ; illustrated by Wayne Geehan.
       p. cm.
Summary: Sir Cumference, Radius, and Sir Vertex search for Edgecalibur,
the sword that King Arthur has hidden in a geometric solid.
    ISBN-13: 978-1-57091-600-7; ISBN-10: 1-57091-600-4 (Reinforced for library use)
    ISBN-13: 978-1-57091-601-4; ISBN-10: 1-57091-601-2 (Softcover)
    1. Mathematics--Juvenile literature. [1. Geometry. 2. Mathematical recreations.] I. Geehan, Wayne, ill. II. Title.
QA40.5.N48 2003
516--dc21
                                          2002153288

One fine morning, Sir Cumference, Lady Di of Ameter, and their son, Radius, sat eating breakfast in King Arthur's castle.

Suddenly, the door flew open and a young knight ran into the room. It was Vertex, Radius's best friend. "I've found out why King Arthur called us all here!" Vertex exclaimed.

3

"The King wants to choose an heir," Vertex explained. "Five knights are competing for the honor. I'm one of them."

"You would make a fine king," Sir Cumference said.

"That's right," agreed Radius. "You helped the King make peace with the Euclideans last year."

"Yes, but now I have to solve the puzzle on this parchment," Vertex said. "The King has hidden his sword, Edgecalibur. The knight who finds it will be the next king."

4

Vertex unrolled a parchment. "This is the only clue the King gave us."

Form the solids and find their places.
How many edges, points, and faces?
The shapes that make two will pass the test,
But one that does not must be your quest.
Three times as tall as its base is wide,
The true King's future lies inside.

"Look at these strange drawings," Lady Di remarked.
"They look like wooden tabletops."

"Let's go ask the carpenters," suggested Radius.
"They know a lot about building tables."

Vertex and Radius ran down to the courtyard. They saw the other knights trying to find Edgecalibur.

One knight was carving solid shapes out of wood. Another knight was counting the edges of each stone in the castle.

A third knight was inspecting the points of several swords. The last knight was looking through schoolbooks for a test with the number two.

7

"I know a shortcut,"
said Radius. He led
Vertex into a tunnel.
"This will take us under the courtyard
to the carpenters' workshop."

The tunnel was dimly lit, and scratching and
squeaking came from the dark shadows.

When they got to the workshop, Vertex showed the carpenters, Geo and Sym of Metry, the drawings on the parchment. "Do you know what these are?" he asked.

"Yes," answered Geo. "These are diagrams showing solid shapes flattened out."

"You can use them to make shapes with height, length, and width," added his brother Sym.

"I see!" nodded Vertex. "Let's try it, Radius."

Vertex and Radius cut and folded the shapes. "The parchment says the shapes that 'make two' will pass the test," Vertex said. "This cube has 6 square sides or faces, 8 corner points, and 12 edges where the faces come together. How do you get a 2 from that?"

"Look at this pyramid," said Radius. "It has 5 faces, 5 points, and 8 edges. I don't see a 2 anywhere."

"Maybe we have to add the number of faces and the number of points," said Vertex. "If we add the pyramid faces and points we get ten. Ten minus the 8 edges is 2."

"Does it work for the cube, too?" asked Radius. "The cube's 6 faces plus its 8 points is fourteen. Fourteen minus the 12 edges is 2. I think you've got it, Vertex!"

Vertex and Radius finished making the shapes. There were cubes, pyramids, rectangular prisms, triangular prisms, cylinders, and cones.

Vertex counted the faces, corner points, and edges of each shape. He added the number of faces and points, then subtracted the number of edges. The answer was 2 each time, except for the cylinder and the cone.

Shape	Flat Faces	Corner Points	Faces + Points	Straight Edges	Faces + Points − Edges
Cube	6	8	14	12	2
Pyramid	5	5	10	8	2
Rectangular Prism	6	8	14	12	2
Triangular Prism	5	6	11	9	2

Vertex unrolled the parchment and read again,

The shapes that make two will pass the test,
But one that does NOT must be your quest.

"The cylinder doesn't have any points, and the cone doesn't have any straight edges. They can't make two and pass the test.

"Our next clue must be a cylinder or cone!" he announced.

"Look at this," said Radius. "I made a model of the castle with the shapes! Here is the pyramid roof on top of the rectangular tower. The other towers are the cylinders with their cone-shaped roofs."

Vertex looked at the model. "Let's search for Edgecalibur in the round towers, since they are built in the shapes of cones and cylinders."

Vertex and Radius climbed up and down the spiral staircase in each round tower. They looked under every trapdoor, in every suit of armor, and behind every tapestry, but there was no sign of Edgecalibur.

"Let's search from above," Vertex said.

They went up to the roof. Vertex had a commanding view of the castle courtyard. "Look at the stones in the path!" he said.

"Each of those round paving stones could be the bottom of a cone or cylinder.

"That path is in the same direction as the tunnel we went through."

17

Vertex and Radius returned to the tunnel. Sharp points jutted down from the ceiling.

"These points could be the tips of cones," Radius said.

"We need to dig them up," said Vertex.

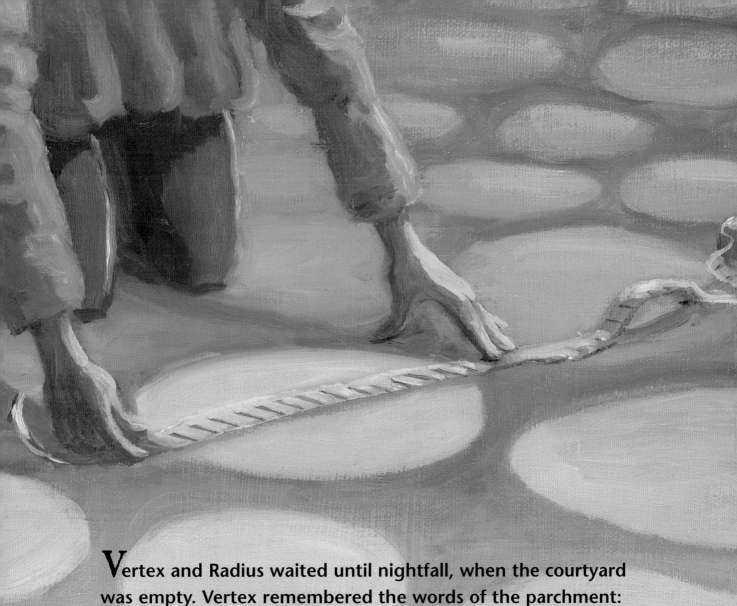

Vertex and Radius waited until nightfall, when the courtyard was empty. Vertex remembered the words of the parchment:

Three times as tall as its base is wide
The true King's future lies inside.

"If the base of a cone is its circular bottom, we need to measure the width of these paving stones." Vertex measured one of the stones. "This cone is 14 inches across its base," he said.

"So it must have a height of 42 inches to be three times as tall," Radius replied.

Vertex and Radius dug up the cone. It was 47 inches high. "Oh, no!" said Radius. "It's more than three times as tall."

"Let's try another one," suggested Vertex. He and Radius dug all night. They unearthed and measured many cones, but none was right. Some were too tall while others were too short.

They still had many cones to go when the full moon set and the day began to dawn.

"We'll never finish," groaned Radius. "We've looked for clues in the tunnel and dug up lots of cones. Where else can we look?"

"We've looked over the cones, under the cones, and on the cones — but what if Edgecalibur is hidden inside a cone?" suggested Vertex. "Are any of them big enough?

"Hmm . . . . Edgecalibur is a sword, so it has to be about 48 inches long, about the same length as this shovel."

Vertex asked, "Radius, will you go back down into the tunnel?"

Soon Vertex heard Radius's voice from below. "I'm in the tunnel, but what am I looking for?"

23

Vertex placed the shovel in the nearest hole. "Can you see any cones that are as long as the shovel?"

"I see four cones that are *about* the same length," Radius answered.

"Edgecalibur could be hidden inside any one of those cones," Vertex said. "But the cone we seek must be three times as tall as its base is wide."

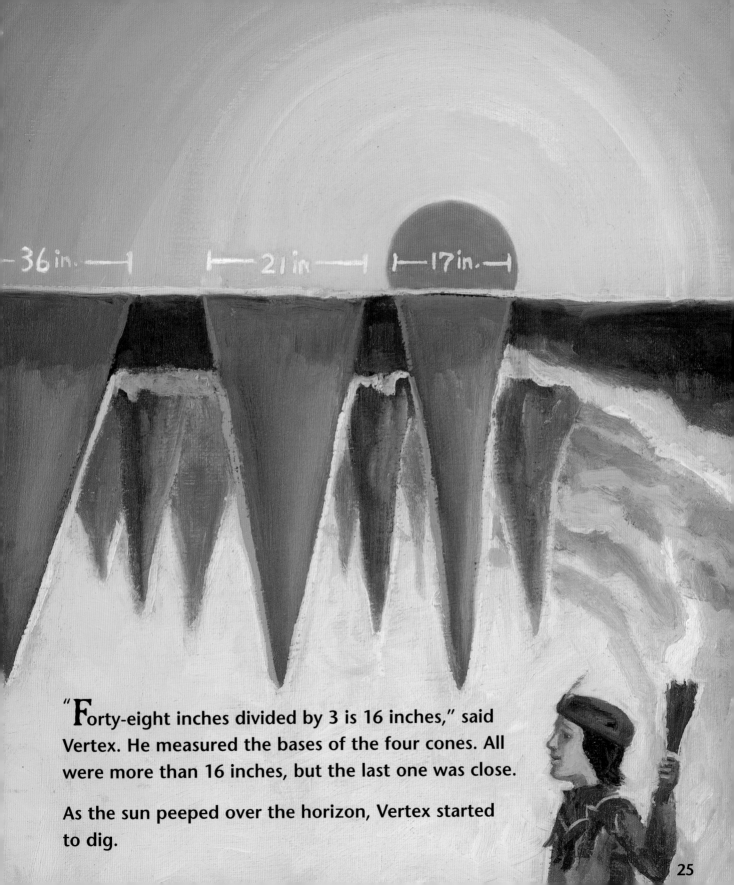

"Forty-eight inches divided by 3 is 16 inches," said Vertex. He measured the bases of the four cones. All were more than 16 inches, but the last one was close.

As the sun peeped over the horizon, Vertex started to dig.

25

Radius ran back up to the courtyard.
Vertex heaved and tugged on the stone.
Finally, he pulled up a large cone.

Vertex measured it. It was
exactly 51 inches high,
three times the 17 inches
of its base!

Vertex pried off the base of the cone and pulled out a gleaming sword.

"Edgecalibur is found!" he exclaimed.

As Vertex held the sword aloft, everyone in the castle came running out. King Arthur said, "You have solved my puzzle, Sir Vertex. Tell us how you used your wit and will to find Edgecalibur."

Vertex bowed low. "Sire," he said, "I folded each of the diagrams on the parchment into a solid shape. Then for each solid I added the number of faces to the number of points and subtracted the number of edges.

"The answer was always 2 until I got to the cylinder and the cone. So Radius and I searched the parts of the castle shaped like cylinders and cones.

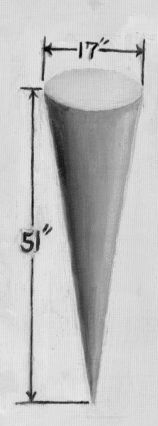

"We found these cones buried in the courtyard. One of them was three times as tall as its base was wide. Edgecalibur was inside."

Vertex knelt and held out the sword.

King Arthur smiled. "Sir Vertex, you have used your intelligence to earn the greatest honor that I can bestow."

The King took Edgecalibur and tapped Vertex on each shoulder. "I dub you Prince Vertex. When I can no longer rule, you shall be King.

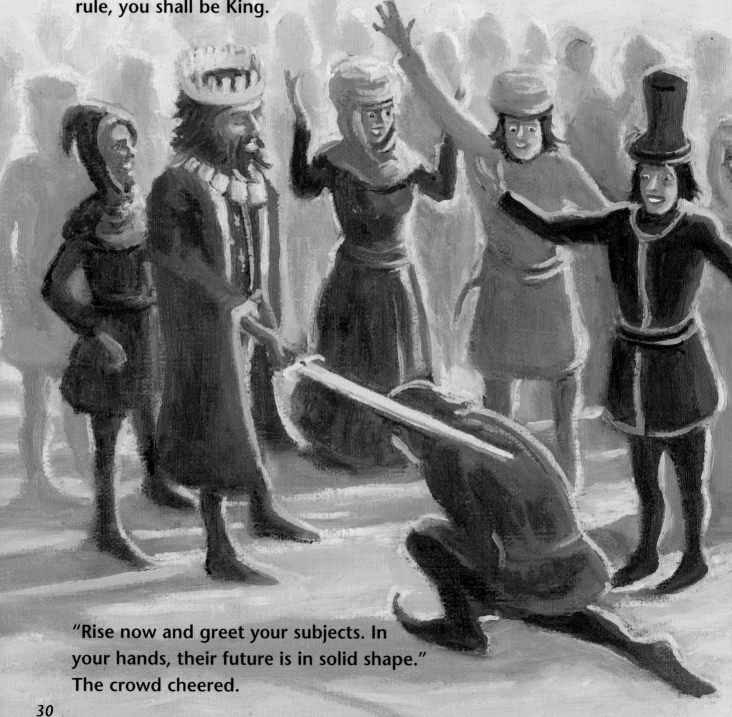

"Rise now and greet your subjects. In your hands, their future is in solid shape." The crowd cheered.

Vertex said, "I want to thank Sir Cumference, Lady Di of Ameter, and Radius. They helped me measure up to the challenge. I hope they will be my advisors when I am King."

Vertex eventually did become a wise and thoughtful king, known to his people as Vertex the Line-Hearted. To this day, the point at the heart of two or more lines is called a vertex.

There really is a mathematical "two's test" for geometric solids. It is called Euler's Law. A Swiss mathematician named Leonhard Euler (OY-ler) (1707-1783) proved in 1751 that if you add the number of faces on a geometric solid to the number of its points (vertices) and then subtract the number of its edges, the answer will always be two. It works for any polyhedron (straight-sided, solid shape).